Lunar
New Year

words&pictures

© 2023 Quarto Publishing Group USA Inc.
Illustrations © Jingting Wang 2023

First published in 2023 by words & pictures,
an imprint of The Quarto Group.
100 Cummings Center,
Suite 265D Beverly,
MA 01915, USA.
T (978) 282-9590 F (978) 283-2742
www.quarto.com

Assistant Editor: Alice Hobbs
Designer: Clare Barber
Production Manager: Nikki Ingram
Art Director: Susi Martin
Associate Publisher: Holly Willsher

A CIP record for this book is available from the Library of Congress.

ISBN: 978-0-7112-8713-6

9 8 7 6 5 4 3 2 1

Printed in Malaysia, COS072023

MIX
Paper | Supporting
responsible forestry
FSC
www.fsc.org
FSC™ C007207

Lunar New Year

illustrated by
Jingting Wang

Natasha Yim

Xin nian hao!

Happy Lunar New Year!
My name is Ling.

My family and I are preparing
for the biggest Chinese festival
of the year. It's a 15-day
holiday where our household
buzzes with activity.

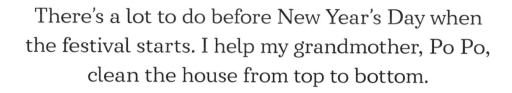

There's a lot to do before New Year's Day when the festival starts. I help my grandmother, Po Po, clean the house from top to bottom.

We sweep away bad luck and evil spirits. When the new year begins, we won't be cleaning for a few days. It could sweep out good luck!

My sister Mei and I dust and polish
the statue of the Kitchen God.
He is the God of the Hearth.
He sits on a shelf in our kitchen,
and watches over our family.

The Kitchen God
reports my family's
activities to the Jade
Emperor in Heaven.

We want him to only
say sweet things, so
it's a custom to paint
honey on his lips.

Mei and I argue about who gets to paint the honey on the Kitchen God's lips. My mom, Ma Ma, reminds us not to quarrel before the new year because it will bring bad luck.

Mei and I agree that we will both brush the Kitchen God's lips. That way, he will have double the sweet things to say about our family.

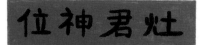

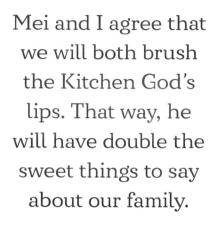

Ma Ma and I pick fresh flowers from our garden. Flowers celebrate the coming of spring and the renewal of life. They bring us happiness and success.

We place them in vases around the house. The fragrant scent of flowers fills our home with sweet perfumes.

We choose pink peonies for peace, red plum blossoms for courage, and fragrant yellow narcissus for good fortune.

My dad, Ba Ba, paints Chinese poems on two long pieces of red paper. Red is the color of good luck. We hang these on either side of our front door. They welcome visitors with wishes for a long life, peace, and great health.

I make red paper cuttings of the Chinese character "fu." It means "fortune" or "luck." We hang these on the front door and windows—upside down! "Upside down" in Chinese sounds like the word for "arrive." So, hanging "fu" upside down means "Your good fortune will arrive."

新春大吉

千花传欢乐

百柳报春兆

13

Now it's time to go shopping. Ma Ma buys us new outfits to wear on New Year's Day.

Po Po buys red lanterns for the Lantern Festival, which is on the last day of the new year celebrations.

We all choose our favorite foods to cook for the reunion dinner on New Year's Eve. Our family will come together to share this delicious holiday meal.

After a week of hard work,
New Year's Eve is finally here!
We honor our ancestors.
We place a roast chicken,
steamed buns, and tangerines
on an altar in front of my
grandfather's picture. He can
have a New Year meal too!

We burn paper versions of gold nuggets, cars, and household goods. The smoke carries these things upwards to Heaven so my grandfather can enjoy them in the afterlife. We light incense sticks and bow three times to show our respect.

Finally, we sit down to eat our reunion dinner. All my aunties, uncles, and cousins are here. The food we eat on this day has special meaning too.

We eat dumplings for wealth, noodles for long life, and turnip cakes for good luck. Round fruits like oranges bring good fortune because they are the shape and color of gold coins. We eat niangao, a sweet, sticky rice cake, in the hope that we will have more of everything good in the coming year. Yum!

On New Year's Day, I put on my new clothes. It's time to visit all our friends and relatives! We bring gifts of tangerines and peach blossoms.

"Gong xi fa cai!"
we say to each other.

Mei and I receive red packets with money inside. The red packets are a wish for happiness and good luck.

Rat-a-tat-a-tat! I can hear firecrackers in the streets. They are very loud. They scare away evil spirits and the new year beast which is called "lien" in Cantonese and "nian" in Mandarin.

Ma Ma told me that according to Chinese legend, a beast used to come down from the mountains and attack the villages every year. A wise man finally drove the beast away with the color red, bright lights, and loud noises. Lunar New Year also celebrates surviving this fearsome beast!

Boom! Boom! Boom! Clang! Clang! Clang! Drums and cymbals announce the New Year's Day parade! Ba Ba carries me on his shoulders so I can see the lion and dragon dancers.

A huge lion head with blinking eyes shimmers and shakes. A red and gold dragon with a long body twists and turns down the street. The longer the dragon, the more good luck it brings.

A fun activity I love to do in the days after New Year's Day is kite-flying. Ba Ba and I take our kites to the park. I have a dragon kite and Ba Ba has one shaped like a rooster.

We float our kites high up in the air and watch as they flutter in the breeze.

The Lunar New Year ends with the Lantern Festival. We hang red lanterns in front of our house.

新春大吉

福

百柳报春兆

Some lanterns glide down nearby ponds or rivers. Some float into the inky night sky.

The glow of the lanterns guides our ancestors back to Heaven, and chases away the darkness. Mei and I carry ours on a stick around the neighborhood.

Some lanterns have riddles taped to them, so Mei and I have fun guessing the answers.

At the Lantern Festival we also eat sweet rice balls filled with fruits and nuts. Their round shapes represent wholeness and togetherness.

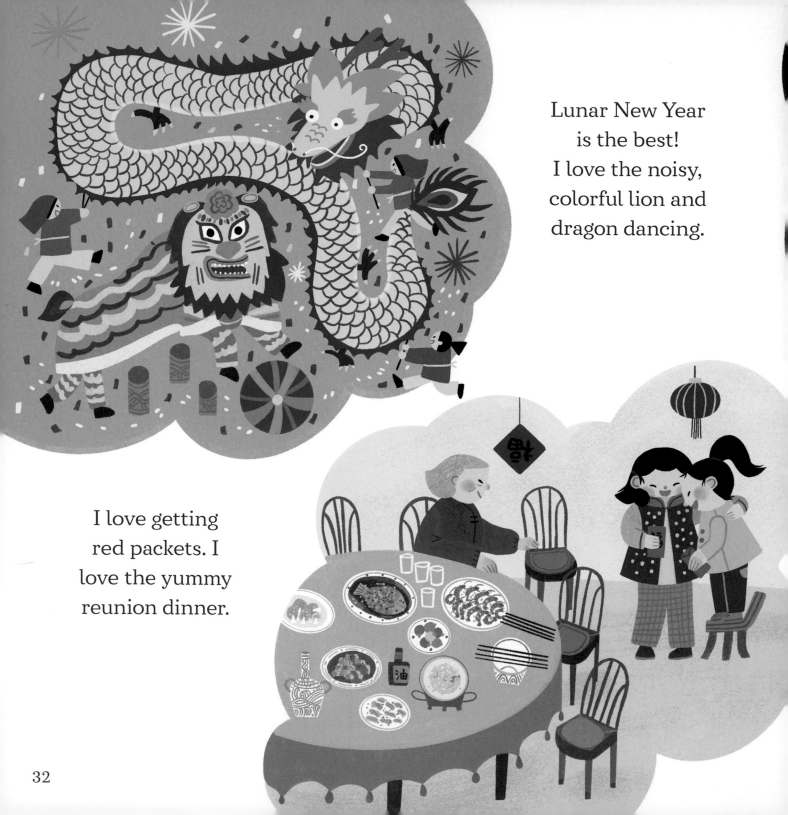

Lunar New Year
is the best!
I love the noisy,
colorful lion and
dragon dancing.

I love getting
red packets. I
love the yummy
reunion dinner.

But most of all,
I love having
my family all
around me.

"Gong xi fa cai,"
everyone! May you
all have good luck
and happiness for
the new year.

Lunar New Year

Lunar New Year is the most important festival of the year for many Asian communities. It is known as the Spring Festival in China, but many Chinese people living around the world call it Chinese New Year. Celebrations usually include firecrackers or fireworks, lion and dragon dancing, gifts, and a New Year feast.

GREETINGS

There are many Chinese languages spoken. Mandarin, the national language of China, is the most widely used. Cantonese is more common in Southern China and in places with large Southern Chinese communities such as San Francisco, California.

Here are some greetings for Lunar New Year in both Mandarin and Cantonese:

Wishing a "Happy New Year" or "New Year Goodness"

Sun nin hou
Sun neen ho
CANTONESE

Xin nian hao
Shing nyen how
MANDARIN

HISTORY OF LUNAR NEW YEAR

Lunar New Year is a very old festival. It dates back to the Shang Dynasty in China which began about 3,500 years ago. Around 1,000 years later, during the Han Dynasty, a yearly date for the festival was set—this was the first day of the first month in the lunar calendar. This usually falls between January 21st and February 20th in the Western calendar.

Wishing someone "Happiness and Prosperity"

Gong xi fa cai
Gong she fa ttsai
MANDARIN

Kung hei fat choi
Gong hay faht choy
CANTONESE

Over 2,000 years ago was also when some Lunar New Year activities began, such as the very first firecrackers! To celebrate, people would burn bamboo which made a loud cracking noise.

The Lunar Calendar and the Chinese Zodiac

Emperor Huangdi, the first emperor of China, is said to have invented the first Chinese calendar over 2,000 years ago.

This calendar followed the phases of the moon and is called the Chinese lunar calendar ("lunar" means moon). Since the phases of the moon fall on different days every year depending on the moon's cycle, Lunar New Year is always on a different date each year.

Which animal are you? To find your animal, look for the year you were born.

PIG

DOG
2018
2006
1994
1982
201
200
19

ROOSTER
2017
2005
1993
1981

MONKEY
2028
2016
2004
1992

GOAT
2027
2015
2003
1991

HORSE
2026
2014
2002

MOUSE

2020
2008
96
1997
4
1985

OX
2021
2009
1986

TIGER
2022
2010
1998

RABBIT
2023
2011
1999
1987

DRAGON
2024
2012
2000
1988

SNAKE

Each year of the lunar calendar is represented by an animal. There are 12 animals in the Chinese zodiac, so each animal's year comes around every 12 years. If you were born in the Year of the Tiger, you'll be twelve years old at the next Tiger year! The order of the animals in the Chinese zodiac is: Mouse, Ox, Tiger, Rabbit, Dragon, Snake, Horse, Goat (or Sheep), Monkey, Rooster, Dog, and Pig.

37

Riddle Activities

The Lunar New Year ends on the 15th day of the first month with the Lantern Festival. It is also the first full moon of the lunar year.

On this day, homes and streets glow with the light of lanterns which are said to guide the ancestors back to Heaven and drive away the darkness. It is also a time when families gather outside to take a stroll in the moonlight with their lanterns, enjoy fireworks and lion dancing, and try to solve riddles attached to the lanterns. Can you solve these riddles?

1. What goes up, but never comes back down?

2. If you drop a yellow hat in the Red Sea, what does it become?

WANT TO CREATE YOUR OWN RIDDLE?
HERE'S HOW:

1. Decide on your answer first.

2. Write down as many words related to your answer as possible. For example, if your answer is "ball," words such as circle, round, and bounce are related. Some things to think about: what does it look like, feel like, sound like? What does your answer do? How is it used? Where do you find it?

3. From the list of words you made, choose 2–4 words.

4. Now, write your own riddle including those words. A few ways you can start your riddle can be: "I am…," "I am not…," "You can use me to…," "I have…"

5. Have fun!

3. I go all around the world, but never leave the corner. What am I?

5. If you drop me, I'm sure to crack, but smile at me, and I'll smile back. What am I?

4. What can you never eat for breakfast or dinner?

Cook Your Own Dumplings

INGREDIENTS:

- 1 pack of pot sticker wrappers
- 1 pound ground pork (you can also use ground beef or a vegetarian alternative)
- 2 scallions or green onions, chopped finely
- $\frac{1}{8}$ teaspoon ground ginger
- 2 tablespoons sesame oil
- 2–3 tablespoons soy sauce
- 1 tablespoon cornstarch or flour
- Sauces of your choice for dipping
- Vegetable oil for cooking

Eating dumplings or pot stickers for Lunar New Year is said to bring money and wealth in the coming year. This is because the shape of the dumplings is like that of ancient Chinese money. You can make your own pot stickers, which are pan-fried dumplings, for Lunar New Year with the help of a grown-up. Here's how:

DIRECTIONS

1. Pop the ground meat and scallions into a bowl. Roll up your sleeves and squish them all together.

2. Add the ground ginger, sesame oil, soy sauce, and cornstarch to the meat. Use a spoon to mix these all together until combined.

3. Spoon 1 teaspoon of the meat filling into the center of a pot sticker wrapper.

4. Wet the edges of the wrapper, and fold it in half, closing the meat filling inside. Press the edges together to seal. You can crimp these edges if you want the pot stickers to be extra special. Use the image as a guide.

5. Ask your grown-up to heat about 2 tablespoons of vegetable oil in a wok or shallow frying pan, then fry the pot stickers on one side until slightly browned.

HOW TO FOLD POT STICKERS

6. While your grown-up is frying, you can prepare the dipping sauce. Pour some soy sauce into your favorite dish. Or combine some of your favorite sauces together to make your own delicious dip. You could use sesame oil, sriracha, rice vinegar, scallions, chili—whatever you like!

7. Ask your grown-up to take the pan off the heat and let it cool a little, then add water to the pan until it covers the bottom half of the pot stickers. Be careful! If the oil is too hot, adding water can make it spatter.

8. Ask your grown-up to bring the water in the pan to a boil, cover the pan with a lid, and then turn the heat to low. They will need to let the pot stickers steam-cook until the water is almost evaporated (about 6–7 minutes). They should then remove the lid and continue to cook the pot stickers until the water completely evaporates and the pot stickers begin to "stick" to the pan.

9. With the help of a grown-up, you can check the bottom of the pot stickers to make sure they are not burning. Ask your grown-up to cook them until they are as brown and crisp as you like.

10. When your grown-up has removed the pot stickers from the hot pan, you can arrange them on a plate and serve them with the dipping sauce you have prepared. Enjoy!

Make a Lucky Envelope

A New Year tradition is to give children a red envelope with money inside. It's good luck to start out the year with some money. Here's how you can make your own "lucky" red envelopes.

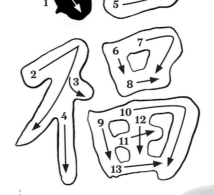

YOU WILL NEED:

- Red paper
- Scissors
- Glue or tape
- Paints, markers, or crayons

DIRECTIONS

1. On a piece of red construction paper, draw out your red envelope template, using the image as your guide. If you do not have red paper, you can use white paper and color it red with a paintbrush and red paint, markers, or crayons.

2. Cut out your envelope along the outside lines.

3. Fold Flap A toward Flap B, using the inside lines. Glue or tape together to seal.

4. Fold Flap C and glue or tape in place. Leave the top flap open.

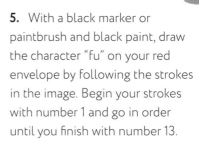

5. With a black marker or paintbrush and black paint, draw the character "fu" on your red envelope by following the strokes in the image. Begin your strokes with number 1 and go in order until you finish with number 13.

6. Now you can put a few coins into your red envelope for good luck, and seal the top flap.

Celebrating Lunar New Year Around the World

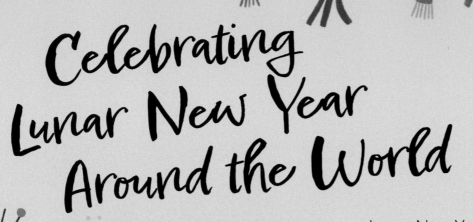

Lunar New Year is also celebrated in other countries around the world, with slightly different traditions and rituals.

For **Koreans**, Lunar New Year is a three-day holiday and is called **Seollal**. A popular food eaten at Seollal is **mandu**, or Korean dumplings. Korean people might also wear the traditional dress called **hanbok** to celebrate the festival.

Lunar New Year may have different traditions in different countries, but they share a few things in common: remembering ancestors, visiting family, and great food.

The **Vietnamese** call their Lunar New Year **Tết**. They eat a special holiday food called **banh chung**—sticky rice filled with meat or bean paste and wrapped in banana leaves.

Another popular New Year food is Vietnamese sausage. Gio is boiled sausage and cha is fried.

In the **Philippines** and for Filipinos around the world, Lunar New Year is celebrated with a midnight feast called **Media Noche**. Right before midnight, children and adults jump up and down so that they'll "grow taller" in the new year.

Quiz

Lunar New Year is an important festival and there are many traditions. Try this quiz to see how much you remember!

Teams of 9 to 15 dancers use long poles to guide the dragon's movements. They dip, sway, and thrust in time to gongs and drums.

1. How long is the Lunar New Year festival?

2. What is one thing people do before New Year's Day?

3. Who is the Kitchen God?

4. How do Mei and Ling get the Kitchen God to say sweet things about their family?

5. What does displaying flowers in the home celebrate?

6. What color is good luck for Lunar New Year?

7. What does the Chinese character "fu" mean?

8. What are some countries that celebrate Lunar New Year?

The Lantern Festival began as a religious festival over 2,000 years ago in the Han Dynasty.

The Lunar New Year meal has special foods that bring good luck.

9. What is the New Year feast called?

10. What is a New Year greeting in Cantonese? What is it in Mandarin?

Answers on the next page!

Answers

RIDDLE ACTIVITIES
1. Your age
2. Wet
3. A stamp
4. Lunch
5. A mirror

QUIZ
1. 15 days
2. Any of these answers: sweep and clean the house, put honey on the Kitchen God's lips, pick flowers, shop for lanterns and new clothes
3. God of the Hearth
4. Paint honey on his lips
5. Coming of spring and renewal of life
6. Red
7. Fortune or luck
8. China, Korea, Vietnam, or the Philippines
9. Reunion dinner
10. Kung Hei Fat Choi or Sun nin hou and Gong Xi Fa Cai or Xin nian hao